Gallery Books
Editor: Peter Fallon

TIME IN ARMAGH

John Montague

"TIME IN ARMAGH"

Gallery Books

Time in Armagh
is first published
simultaneously in paperback
and in a clothbound edition
on 30 June 1993.

The Gallery Press
Loughcrew
Oldcastle
County Meath
Ireland

ISBN 1 85235 112 8 (*paperback*)
    1 85235 113 6 (*clothbound*)

The Gallery Press receives financial assistance from An Chomhairle
Ealaíon / The Arts Council, Ireland, and acknowledges also the assis-
tance of the Arts Council of Northern Ireland in the publication of this
book.

Contents

for Gerry Wrixon,
a sustaining friend

Preface

The scene is St. Patrick's College, Armagh, the time 1941-1946, during the last war. Armagh is the ecclesiastical capital of Ireland, the seat chosen by Patrick for his bishopric, and the old Protestant Cathedral sleeps on a hill in the middle of the town, outfaced by the triumphalist neo-Gothic of the new Catholic Cathedral. So ancient history and modern history crossed, as the German planes wandered over Ulster, where the Invasion armies were assembling. But we were forbidden the radio or the papers.

And our small souls were being regimented by the Vincentian Order, whose main task was to produce priests for the Armagh diocese. I do not think I could exaggerate the harshness of our schooling: while there is a fine account of such conditions in Joyce's *Portrait of the Artist*, Clongowes was already a posh school, and not a junior seminary. The best comparison would probably be with a military academy, the ragging, the fagging, the almost ritual beatings, by one's own contemporaries, as well as the priests. I give a picture of it in 'That Dark Accomplice' from *Death of a Chieftain* (1964), but the story was more complicated than that, the cruelty, the compelled chastity, the ignorant isolation. I do not blame the priests, for whom we were God-fodder, nor my classmates, because we all had to survive. But at an age when tenderness was needed we got none, and learnt to hide human weakness. And over it all the great bell rang every quarter.

A free style is out of the question: this is your old-style Catholic schooling, all the way back to medieval times. It is no accident that I hover near the *canzone* of Dante, as well as the sonnet; the material was already shaped into strict forms by the discipline of the school. The only disruptive element might have been love, but that was an absence. We fantasized about the sisters of younger boys, and film stars, but never saw real girls, except the skivvies who waited on the tables, and Matron who fed us dollops of cod-liver oil.

Periodically boys were expelled for indecency; but we never discussed our bodies, except in confession. It is tempting to think that this was the last period of a typical Catholic boarding-school education, and that the great events happening in the outside world would hasten change in our little one.

I, too, drew my hand back from the cane.
— Juvenal

Guide

Heavy bells that rang above my head,
Sounds loneliness distilled
When Frank Lenny led me, gentle guide,
Under the Cathedral shade
And the gross carillon stirred.

Sick again, I had arrived months late
To hear the shoal's
Seashell roaring along the corridors
While my old neighbours
Fell silent in the cold parlour.

Garvaghey and Glencull were fleeing,
Leaving me to float,
A stray leaf, down the furious whirlpool
Of a junior seminary
From dawn Mass to Gaelic football.

Cowering at the dark soutane's swirl
Along the study hall;
Harder still, in the long dormitory's chill,
The midnight patrol
With probing torch, and cane's swish!

The holy war against the growing body
In the name of chastity;
Dean Mack peering over my writing shoulder
Into my first diary:
'Any little girls' names there, have we?'

Would there had been a warm-breasted army!
Dear Frank Lenny,
For you, the flesh never raised a difficulty,
As you led us all
In solemn procession towards the Cathedral,

Satin-surpliced, with white gloves to uphold
The train of the cardinal.
Pageboy, Head Prefect, ordained priest,
Your path was straight:
One of their own, a natural for the episcopate.

Who would not envy such early certainty?
Across your celibate's bed
You fell last year, gone early upwards
Towards the heavens
Which, steadfast, you still believed in.

If, late again, I arrive flaunting my rival beliefs,
My secular life,
Will you be there, to greet and guide me,
White-gloved, gentle,
Proud of our Tyrone accent, my boyhood Virgil?

Retreat, 1941

Early into the first term, a weekend retreat
To seal our barely stirring senses off.
(The Wehrmacht stalls before Stalingrad.)
Wartime rations already made a meagre diet,
Yet, skin pitted with boils, hands chilblained,
We still had to mortify our sinful appetites
With black sugarless tea, white butterless bread.

Silence as well as hunger was an obligation.
Around the Junior/Senior Rings we marched,
Monkish recruits, eyes lowered, or cowed
Heads bowed into edifying texts, after sermons
Where a Passionist preacher raged against temptation.
Daniel A. Lord on *Keeping Company with Women*
Before we had a chance to get around to them!

A Bomber's Moon

Then there were the terrible nights when Belfast was bombed and stray planes of the Luftwaffe penetrated as far as Armagh. One crossed low over the tossing trees at the end of the football field: we could hear the engine's roar as it swooped. Crouched in the dampness of the hastily constructed air-raid shelters we awaited the shudder, the flash, the quick moment of extinction.

'Oh, Lord,' I prayed, on my knees at the leaf-strewn entrance, 'let me not feel death, only die so suddenly that I will not know what it is all about.'

The air seemed to quiver with the upward beat of wings as the plane zoomed over the school buildings and away, leaving the frightened boys staring at the sky, the silvered spires of the Cathedral; moonlit nights were best for bombing raids. In that moment he had known everything; the possibility of death, in the shape of a dark angel, something apocalyptic and avenging as the images conjured up in a Lenten sermon in the chapel. Then the rising wail of the All Clear.

'It's gone . . . . '

In the candle- and torch-lit darkness of their concrete cave the boys turned frightened heads upwards, no longer in fear, but in thanksgiving.

'It's gone,' they chorused.

Father Rafferty, their favourite priest, blessed himself again, and began to lead the Rosary, with relief, in the blessèd silence of the raid's aftermath.

'Come now, boys, let us all kneel down and pray to the Blessed Virgin, in thanks for having been saved, this time.'

As he knelt, running the beads through his fingers with practised skill, he was aware of some menace, at the edge of his retina. From his vantage point he could see that, although they themselves were safe and sound, the stain on the Eastern sky was growing, like a bloodshot eye.

'Let us pray,' he said to himself, 'for all the poor people of Belfast.'

Openings

1 *Peeping Tom*

Among the pious mottoes
of a flower-wreathed album,
Remember me when this you see
And we are far apart.
Remember me on bended knee
Before the Sacred Heart,

Tom Campbell inserts
his chivalric sentiment:
I have a dainty girlfriend
And this you'll comprehend,
Every time she bends her knee
I see the Promised Land.

Dean Mack, on the prowl,
saw the Fires of Hell,
and chubby, friendly Campbell
expelled for indecency.

His father arrives immediately,
declaring he was delighted
to take his normal son away
from such senseless hypocrisy.

2 *Peephole*

Behind and above our bowed heads
At the end of the long study hall
Was a viewing window, a Judas hole,
To spy on the mischief we were up to;
Caherty acting the maggot as usual,
Montague or Muldoon gabbling,
John Donaghy studying racing form.
Once John and I made a stink bomb
(A test tube of sulphuric acid and iron)
Which swiftly cleared out that hated room.
One of the best experiments I have done:
Spying on people is obscene. Besides, alas,
The only opening left was our imagination,
Sulphurous laughter our only weapon.

Special Intentions

Lonely hours before the altar,
Heads bow in palms, as a battery of prayers
Assaults heaven, for our Special Intentions.

Please God, help me pass the exam.
St. Joseph, get me onto the school team.
Blessèd Mediatrix, intercede with the Dean
Not to beat me so much, this next term.

Did holy answering presences hover
Over the long dormitory of hidden tears,
Of scarred knees, welted palms, sore ears,
Or, most shaming of all, secret fears?

The confessor's crouched ear, raised palm:
'Did you draw fluids from your body again?'
A heavy sigh: 'Madness grows from self-pollution.'
The warm, vague seawash of absolution.

Nightly the Cathderal beat its iron tune
Over youth's humiliations, its growing pains;
Mouse rustle of sheets where bodies burn.

Extra Mural

for William Smyth

Once a week, the Sunday walk brought us back outside
the walls, *extra muros*, in orderly formation. There was
the Geography Walk, led by our most mild master, the
Reverend Mickey Block. His real name, Rafferty, I
remember with difficulty; we certainly thought he had a
beam missing. He droned on happily about the drumlins
that had formed Armagh, a scatter of little eggshaped hills
deposited by the Ice Age: the two Cathedrals which
confronted each other across the city were founded on
drumlins. He might be daft on drumlins but he also doted
on terminal moraines and river basins, like the Boyne,
and loved to draw the loops of an oxbow, meanders
created by rough ground which the insistent river slow-
nudged. The Moy had an oxbow lake like the Mississippi
which spelt aloud was a snake slithering, with a hiccup.
Did anyone live in a townland with an esker? I put up my
hand: Eskra was next door to Garvaghey.

Coniferous and deciduous trees clung to or lost their
leaves in winter, stalactites and stalagmites fell from or
rose to the rooves of caves, mountains folded and buckled
into synclines and anticlines: the earth was a living
theatre. Chosen pupils crept across the lawn on an impor-
tant mission every morning, to consult the rain gauge set
in the grass near the Senior Walk, a step away from the
trees. The water collected overnight was measured in a
graduated cylinder, and the results entered into a logbook
beside the barograph with its moving pen which traced
the line of pressure in millibars. Dear Mickey Block, he
kept us amused and busy with his dreams: his stocky little

figure would stop before some rushy gap while he conjured up, with oblivious eloquence, some lost glory that we could barely see. Rumour (school's private waveband) had it that he was arrested as a spy while pottering around during the Long Vac, making sketches of areas used for Allied War manoeuvres. Anyway, at the end of Second Year, he did not come back.

Fraternal Love

1

Reared by loving, long-suffering aunts
I learnt in this academy of hard knocks
how God protects the sensitive plant.

Rough Hugh from a cow town near home
who sat behind me, did damn all work
but beat a brisk tattoo upon my bum.

Next night, an apology would come,
slyly passed along the cold study hall.
Please John, I know I did wrong

but can I copy down your sums
or I'll be in the soup? I've nothing
done, and I'll be hauled before the Dean.

A loyal idiot, I always gave in,
hoping kindness would stem his sadism
but he thrived upon it. Next time

we meet, *I'll be dug out of him,*
I often thought, but when I found him,
whiskey sodden, claiming old affection,

I gave in, again. So an earlier pattern
was confirmed. Life, which had almost broken
Hugh's hold on anything, tightened Borman's!

2

Big Borman coralled me in a room
to beat me black and blue. Jumbo then
sought to make amends, slobbering

as he grappled, *I really love you.*
Now a Canon, with his own parish,
and very well-liked. At least Hugh

went back to the cattle-dealing!
And what if I met the other shagger?
Now that he sports the sacerdotal black

and can absolve our mortal errors,
the best I might manage to stammer
is that nights I still try to forgive

his puffy, clumsy reign of terror.

Lunatic

Screwy, or *Nuts*, they called me,
Because of my hawk, or handsaw, stance.
I would treat nothing seriously
Where all was harsh, boorish, ignorant.
Sated with small cruelties, I soon learnt
To sing dumb, or pull a loony face;
An antic disposition, my best defence.
My best advance, to leap exams like hurdles
Towards the fabled world of films and girls.
Once I doffed my jester's cap and bells
To front a hunger-strike, a mute rebellion.
To see Dean Mack flinch was brief recompense,
The soon palling pleasure of the dark accomplice:
Good pupils, grown just as mean as them.

Time in Armagh

1

Hazing, they call it in America,
but I already knew it from Armagh,
the fledgeling hauled to the pump,

protesting, by the bigger boys
to be baptised with his nickname,
Froggy, *Screwy*, *Rubberneck* or *Dopey*,

some shameful blemish, his least attract-
ive aspect, hauled out to harry, haunt him
through his snail years in St. Patrick's,

a five-year sentence. Even in the chapel
in that hush of prayers and incense
the same cruelty was ritually practised,

shoving the prongs of the dividers
into the thighs of the smaller boy
who knelt before you. He couldn't cry

in such a sacred atmosphere, disturb
the priest murmuring on the altar,
the tinkle for the lofted Eucharist.

Sometimes, they used a Sacred Heart pin
to jab the victim. Tears spilt down
his face, while the Blessed Virgin

smiled inside the altar rails, and
Christ stumbled from station to station
around our walls, to His crucifixion,

thorn spiked, our exemplary victim.

2

Then there was the gym and Gaelic football,
both compulsory. Dopey hid down a manhole
to escape these Spartan training sessions

where his slower wits betrayed him
to more jibes and taunts. He held on
but thirty years later, a grown man,

he began to break down, a boy, weeping,
plunged in the pit again, long hours waiting
in that damp darkness, until he heard

the thud of studded boots above his head.

3

Endless games designed to keep us pure —
'Keep your hands out of your pockets, boys' —
we wore togs even in the showers.

No wonder Donaghy fired a brick through
a window when he left. 'I loathed every hour,
every minute,' wrote Des from Bangor,

'what you learnt was to be a survivor.
Remember our eccentric English music master;
what you need is a jolly good six-ah!'

Which, gentle soul, he never administered.
But those of the order of Melchisedech
were no slouches when it came to the stick.

Father Roughan, all too rightly named,
had a fine selection of swishing canes,
test-lashing the air before he landed one

right down the middle of the open palm,
or tingling along the shaking fingertips,
until the hand was ridged with welts.

Dismissed, the boys tried to hide
and hug their hurt under the armpits,
not a whimper, until safely outside

where the cub pack huddled around them,
offering the cold comfort of admiration:
sudden conspiracy of bully and victim

united before the black-skirted enemy.
Our stiff upper lip was an Ulster clamp.
No whingeing. No quarter for the crybaby.

Still to this late day, I rage blind
whenever I hear that hectoring tone,
trying to put another human being down.

The guilt givers who know what is right,
they can shove their rules. A system
without love is a crock of shite.

Waiting

Halting in Dungannon between trains
We often wandered outside town
To see the camp where German
Prisoners were kept. A moist litter
Of woodshavings showed
Ground hastily cleared, and then —

The huge parallelogram
Of barbed wire, nakedly measured
And enclosed like a football field
With the guard towers rising, aloof
As goalposts, at either end.

Given length and breadth we knew
The surface area the prisoners paced
As one hung socks to dry outside
His Nissen hut, another tried
To hum and whistle *Lili Marlene*:
They seemed to us much the same

As other adults, except in their
Neutral dress, and finding it normal
To suffer our gaze, like animals,
As we squatted and pried, for an hour
Or more, about their human zoo

Before it was time for shopfronts,
Chugging train, Vincentian school.
A small incident, soon submerged
In our own brisk, bell-dominated rule:
Until, years later, I saw another camp —
Rudshofen, in the fragrant Vosges —

Similar, but with local improvements:
The stockade where they knelt the difficult,
The laboratory for minor experiments.
The crematorium for Jews and gypsies
Under four elegant pine towers, like minarets.

This low-pitched style seeks exactness,
Daring not to betray the event.
But as I write, the grid of barbed
Wire rises abruptly around me,
The smell of woodshavings plugs
My nostrils, a carrion stench.

Red Hat

The Cardinal's hat, tasselled, wide-brimmed
as a ringed planet, futuristic flying saucer
or satellite, was our school arms,
an emblem sported on navy cap and blazer
and as crest on our school writing paper,
embossed with a motto, *Dominus dat Sapientiam*,
to dignify our little Papish dungeon.

The Lord might give wisdom, indeed,
to small boys emulating a British code,
but the only time we paid much heed
to bushy browed Cardinal MacRory was when —
dramatically announced in the chapel at dawn
by our President, old Brass Jaws Sheridan —
we won a week's holidays, because he was dead.

Deo Gratias

I bribed Caherty with a Mars Bar
a day to replace me at the High Altar.
Our college oratory was being painted:
scaffoldings, buckets between the Stations
of the Cross, the canvas draped statues.
So we had been allotted the morning run
of Armagh Cathedral, and it was my turn
to mumble back the Latin responses.

Checked and choked by my stammer,
how could I serve our houseled Lord
in such *a halting, disagreeable manner*?
I recalled a funeral service at home,
every response dragging like a chain
'till a weary priest took over: *humiliation*.

Dean Roughan spotted my weak trick,
summoned me to his study, canes racked
near the door, beneath a chilling text
in block letters: NO FUN LIKE WORK.
A Senior, I was offered the choice —
a public caning or to raise my voice
again next week, which would be High Mass.

The brisk Dean had forgotten that to sing,
albeit tunelessly, is possible to the stammering.
Father MacCurtain, who quavered *Panis Angelicus*
in his high tenor at our school concerts,
was the celebrant. Moon-faced old Mack

was a good sort, bending over the tabernacle,
then turning to smile sly encouragement
as we began to intone our formal chant.

Slowly, the whole school joined warmly in:
the high vault rang with grave Gregorian.

Father Kangaroo

for Mark

Our lean bespectacled Australian Classics master
Made us insert a blank sheet of paper
Over the reproduction of naked statues
In our slim *Daily Life in Ancient Rome*,
— thus drawing our sniggering attention to them.

The fig-leaved powers of great Hercules
Or some Virgilian hero, Turnus or Aeneas:
A fullback with no togs or jersey on him!

The smooth marble buttocks and calm
Breasts of a goddess, Aphrodite/Venus:
Matron, without a stitch on her!

Our bleak refectory became the *triclinium*
But what we liked best was the *vomitorium*.
Old Kangaroo never guessed what was going on
As we cheerfully conjugated *Amo, amas, amat*,
Or declined among Masc., Fem., Neut.,
With more in our heads than the Ablative Absolute.

History Walk

Our History Master was a curly headed young priest who leaned too close to us in class, the better to inspect our copybooks, *moryah*. Often I felt his downy cheek press against mine, though I doubt if he knew what he was doing: he was as ignorant and naive as the rest of us. Yet he could be enthusiastic; in our first term, before the official N.I. Syllabus swallowed us, we learnt about something called Early Irish Civilisation. I loved it, Larne flints, osiered banquet halls, the bronze trumpet of Lough na Shade. *Then it was back to the origins of the Industrial Revolution.*

Once myth and reality warmly met, when we swarmed over Navan Fort. Sheep grazed where Cuchulain and his High King, Conor, argued, a quarry ate the grass where Deirdre first saw her young warrior. But we were doing English and Modern History for our State exams, not Irish, so the mythic figures melted into the mizzling rain, the short views returned: we were standing on a large green hillock in the County Armagh, Northern Ireland, not on the magic mound of Emain Macha, the hillfort of the Red Branch knights. *There would surely be a question on William Pitt, and the Corn Laws.*

History Walks were rarer than Geography, perhaps because they feared to disturb our local nest of pismires. History lay about us in our infancy, with many levels, but only one stratum open. They did not have to explain to us why our new Cathedral had been built on a higher hill. We explored our ancient rival when we ran footloose through town. We marvelled at its echoing emptiness, the rotting flags of Imperial wars. The roll call in the side chapel of the Royal Irish Fuseliers might have taught us something; O's and Macs mingled in death with good Proddy names, Hamilton, Hewitt, Taylor, Acheson.

Instead we ran down the curling, cobbled hill, giggling with guilt. Doomed as any Armada, the lost city of Ard Macha coiled in upon itself, whorl upon whorl, a broken aconite. Layer upon layer had gone to its making, from Cuchulain to St. Patrick, from fleet-footed Macha to Primate Robinson's gaggle of Georgian architects. But the elegance of the Mall was of no avail against simple-minded sectarianism; Armagh, a maimed capital, a damaged pearl.

We sensed this as we sifted through the shards in the little County Museum. Bustled around the glass cases by Curly Top, we halted before a Yeoman's coat, alerted by our party song, 'The Croppy Boy'. And we read about the battle of Diamond Hill between 'Peep-o'-Day Boys' and Catholic Defenders which led to the founding of the Orange Order at Loughgall, a canker among the apple blossoms.

We did not discuss this in our History Class, which now dealt with the origins of the First World War, from the shot in Sarajevo. It did crop up in R.K., Religious Knowledge, where the Dean warned us against the dangers of Freemasonry. A Catholic could never become King of England or President of the United States; everywhere the black face of Protestantism barred the way to good Catholic boys. Amongst the cannon on the Mall the Protestant boys played cricket, or kicked a queer shaped ball like a pear. According to my Falls pal Protestant balls bounced crooked as the Protestants themselves. One day that banter would stop when a shot rang out on the Cathedral Road.

A Human Smile

for Finn

In trim blazers, beneath the shadow
of the new Cathedral, we paraded
in a slow crocodile, down Armagh town

Through Irish, English, Scotch Street,
nametags of our Northern metropolis;
the old Cathedral glooming over us.

Two by two, bright boots and shoes,
arms swinging, eyes fixed before,
small soldiers of the religious wars

We marched primly past Protestant boys
sauntering down from the Royal School.
Then — a tactical error — one day we crossed

A more unnerving race. All the girls
streaming down from the convent, uniforms
as well, but sporting pert looks, curls

That threatened to disrupt our column.
The Prefects had to give a signal.
One (a future bishop) raised his cap.

Sheepishly, we followed that gracious sign.
For one split second, grim habit's crocodile
blinked, risked a human smile.

Absence

One by one, the small boys nod off.
The only light left, my Prefect's torch.
For an hour I have patrolled the dorm,
Checking that Romeo Forte is not snoring,
That Gubby Lenny is not homesick, weeping,
The terrible O'Neill twins not whispering.
Surely Dean Roughan will not do the rounds
Tonight, so I have a chance to warm up again
My letter to a convent girl in Lurgan,
Concealed inside my Modern History volume.
I can still smell the fragrance of your hair,
Your small ears, like seashells, and so on.
The water pipes knock, the great bells sound.
To the chill dark of my cubicle I summon
The sweet blessing of a girlish presence,
Shaping my lips to kiss her absence.

A Lesser Species

for George Watson

Day boys, a different breed, a lesser species,
Who had not spent their time in the trenches.

We grudged their going home to a warm fry
And a soft bed with, perish the thought,
An unmanning kiss from one of their parents!

Despising, we still learnt to use them,
Guerrillas, ferrying Crunchy and Mars Bars,
And later, of course, love's messengers.

Conch

for Tom Redshaw

On the brown polished wood of our parlour sideboard
rested a large rose and cream seashell. Some traveller's
trophy, Uncle Thomas on his way to and from the
Missions, a visitor from Australia or America. Turreted
and spiky, it seemed the seaside palace of some mollusc,
disturbed from its living sleep on a distant strand. When I
was on my own, I picked it up, sliding my hand around the
cold smooth flange, trying to reach into its pink interior.
But my reach was too short.

They said that if you listened to its hidden heart or lung
you could hear the sea's roar. I cupped my ear against it,
again and again, and dreamt that I heard a distant, gentle
humming, the air whistling, perhaps, in that dark, secret
interior. But the ocean at Bundoran was louder, especially
when the waves pounded Roguey Rocks and the spume flew.

One day I carried it outside, to the hill behind our house,
and held it in the air. Now the sound was louder and
stronger, a groan more than a whistle, as the wind poured
through. On impulse, I raised the jagged orifice, the
broken end, to my lips, and managed to blow a low, slow
note.

Then from my solitary reading I remembered what it
was, a conch, a marine shell or spiral, sometimes used as a
trumpet, a slughorn. Roland at Roncevaux, Ulysses calling
his men back to ship, I raised it again. Our cattle turned
their heads slowly, a surprised swallow dived by. Each
year, as my fingers reached further into the curl of the
spiral, took a firmer grasp of its creamy mantle, my note
grew stronger.

Great Root

'Thou art a perpetual triumph, an everlasting bonfire-light'
— Henry IV, Part I

Jock's nose was wondrous to behold,
Jock's nose was a blazing, blaring beacon,
Jock's nose was a flaring human torch,
Which all of us dream-longed to touch.

Last in his class, a duffer at games,
He still ferried the Olympic flame
Of his ancestral nasal appendage,
To which we proferred mock heroic homage.

A Celtic Glaswegian, nigh a simpleton,
He heard himself hailed as O Great One,
Salamander Bardolph, Chief Rising Sun,
His blemish kindled into a blessing.

Or, at least, a pressing. Like a prince
He learnt to lower his huge proboscis
So that its soft pulp might be caressed,
Rubbed reverently, by any commoner

Adoring the great serpent, or royal sceptre.

The Prophet

Solemnly marching around the Junior Ring,
an innocent from my lost townland,
dogged as his boots. The wags crowd
about him, snigger at his conversation;
discoursing dolefully, like a weatherman:

Boys, a sky like that, bound to rain.
Skillfully, the townies teased him,
posing queries about wind and grain.
His grave prophecy: *Tomorrow, it'll turn,*
made a fresh crop of giggles sprout again.

In the dormitory they discovered
his trunk, our old American one,
ran on castors. Like a toy train
they rode it up and down, himself
pleading behind: *Now leave that alone.*

One night he broke down, blubbering.
I had to halt it, warming the lugs
of one big cub, the ringleader, and
then another, till they backed down.
Still Garvaghey plodded oblivious on

Above the swirling sounds of Armagh town,
the Bambrook children droning their lessons,
the unemployed singing *I'll take you home again . . . .*
Tiring of the joke, they called him the Prophet,
but for the weather, left him trudge alone.

Rounds

The Junior Ring was a small plateau on a slope above Bambrook, the poorer part of town. On one side bulked the handball alleys, tall as prison walls; on the other, the stinks of the redbrick Chemistry lab. Although the sounds of the town drifted up, especially in the evening, the outside world was fading away. We spoke in hushed tones about the Seniors, those tall heroes whose doings were so distant and awesome, although each step was bringing us towards them. 'Will Iggy Jones be Captain next year?' 'I'd rather be a footballer any day than a dab,' said John 'Buns' Kennedy to me; he was neither.

Round and round we went, like horses in a pound, talk of home diminishing, as the College took over our lives, the small world driving out the larger. By Third Year we neither glanced down nor listened to the sounds outside. Only the crack of an ace striking a butt, like a pistol shot, or the clang of the handbell, calling us to class or church or the high barn of the refectory.

Now we were heading for the brisk compactness of Senior Ring, with its view of the primatial Cathedral, and the Cardinal's House, *Ara Coeli*. Perhaps one of our lot would end up there one day, sporting the Red Hat: stranger things had happened. On Senior Ring more serious subjects were canvassed, as we discussed our now looming futures, in the light of the *summum bonum*. Particular friendships were not encouraged so we marched in groups of three, or four, or five; only football rivalled religion and exams in the round of our ruminations. Most of the class were going to be priests, changing one uniform for another as they marched through the wide front gate.

I kept my weather eye on the little wicket gate to one side, which led directly to the town. Soon I was skipping study, pretending to be sick, and slipping down to see Claudette Colbert in a bath of milk, Betty Grable's pyramid of peroxided hair, and pin-up gams, the contraband excitement of Movietone News. Years later, when I saw the diagram for Yeats's gyres, I thought of the Junior and Senior Rings, the narrowing funnel of Junior Ring, the widening circle of Senior.

You did in your eye; you tried never to think of them again as soon as you were shut of them.

Goals

Below the school, two football fields,
Two pairs of goalposts, echoing the twin spires'
Proclamation: there are goals loftier than scholarship.

Our early target, Ulster's MacRory Cup,
Then 'Sail Armagh down the field,' all the way
To Croke Park, the first Colleges Championship.

Jim Devlin at fullback, Iggy Jones up front:
His quicksilver runs rattle the goal net:
V-E and V-J Day seemed far less important.

Goalkeeper Caherty went AWOL from our billet,
Spent the night at a lurid Fairview carnival,
Where under the whirling lights he met a girl.

At breakfast grinning: *the goalie scores a goal*.

A Welcoming Party

Wie war das möglich?

That final newsreel of the war:
A welcoming party of almost shades
Met us at the cinema door
Clicking what remained of their heels.

From nests of bodies like hatching eggs
Flickered insectlike hands and legs
And rose an ululation, terrible, shy;
Children conjugating the verb 'to die'.

One clamoured mutely of love
From a mouth like a burnt glove;
Others upheld hands bleak as begging bowls
Claiming the small change of our souls.

Some smiled at us as protectors.
Can those bones live?
Our parochial brand of innocence
Was all we had to give.

To be always at the periphery of incident
Gave my childhood its Irish dimension; drama of unevent:
Yet doves of mercy, as doves of air,
Can falter here as anywhere.

That long dead Sunday in Armagh
I learnt one meaning of total war
And went home to my Christian school
To belt a football through the air.

Vigil

On the first Thursday of every month
The sirens sound through the city
A warning exercise. It begins
With the sobbing call of the Alert
Which, against my will, seems
A nostalgic, almost homely sound
Recalling nights at Armagh school
When, cramped in cold shelters,
We heard planes prowling overhead,
Saw, across Belfast, the night sky
Swollen with fire, like blood.

That is the real border, the grit
Of different experience, of shared terror
No swift neutral sympathy can allay.
Only the rising pulse of the All Clear
Cleanses, permits the day.

Outside Armagh Jail, 1971

Shelley hectic from a sickness,
I arrive twenty-four hours late,
driven from Belfast by two Lyric
stage assistants. Mary O'Malley warns,
Please John, don't involve them:
Theatrically, I never mix with politics.
They carefully explain, on the way down,
that they are liberal: *about as Protestant*
as you are Catholic; not fanatic, *heartsick.*

And then Armagh, its calm Georgian Mall.
A student's memory of bells, the carillon
echoing from the new Cathedral, glooms
over the old walls and sleeping cannon,
the incongruously handsome Women's Prison.
By the railings, two impassive R.U.C. men.
I ring formally and ask for Bernadette:
an incredulous giggle and a slammed door
is the iron answer that I get.

Exposed on the steps like Seanchan,
I intone the scop stresses of my Derry poem.
Lines of suffering/lines of defeat.
One of the constables shifts his feet,
the other is grinning broadly. A secret
acolyte of poetry? I can hear him
rubbing his hands in the guardroom;
Boys, that was great crack! The Fenians
must be losing. This time they sent a lunatic.

Stone

Cathedral,
I shape you in the air with my hands,
On a night when a cutting wind
Counts the hours
With chill bursts of rain.

Cathedral,
Tall-spired guardian of my childhood
In the Ulster night,
Over Saint Patrick's city
The rooves are eyelashed with rain

As the iron bell
Swings out again, each quarter's notes
Dwindling down a shaft of past
And present, to drown
In that throat of stone.

I lived in Armagh in a time of war,
The least conscious time of my life.
Between two stones may lie
My future self
Waiting that you pass by.

If she pass by,
Dislodging the stone of my youth,
Cathedral,
Enclosure and cloister, prow of lost surety,
Resound for me!

Acknowledgements

More than any other book of mine, many friends have helped with this volume, some survivors of similar regimens. I was guided back to Armagh by my cousin, George, given a title by Mícheál Ó Siadhail, went through the first manuscript with Mark Waelder in Syracuse, the last in Cork with Tony Sheehan. Scholars and poets, Richard Bizot, Barry Callaghan, David Coleman, Theo Dorgan, Peter Fallon, Adrian Frazier, David Lampe, George and Gerry Watson of Portadown, Gerry Wrixon, all cast a warm eye. And not men only: Finn O'Gorman told me of her parallel days in Armagh Convent, and Joan MacBreen commiserated. The Gagens and Smiths offered warm hospitality in the Albany snows as I worked and, finally, Tom Redshaw and the ghost of Ponge prodded me to more prose poems. I am grateful to them all and to *Éire-Ireland*, *Poetry Ireland Review* and *Ploughshares* where some of these poems appeared.